LETTERRS

T0126441

LETT*ERR*S

Orlando White

NIGHTBOAT BOOKS
NEW YORK

© 2015 by Orlando White
All rights reserved
Printed in the United States
2nd Printing, 2023

ISBN 978-1-937658-35-9

Design and typesetting by Margaret Tedesco
Text set in DTL Fleischmann

Cover image wrap: Emmi Whitehorse
S.O., 2008. Oil on paper on canvas
Courtesy of the artist

Author photo: Layli Long Soldier

Cataloging-in-publication data is available from the Library of Congress

Nightboat Books
New York
www.nightboat.org

For Chance Ohitika White & Sherwin Bitsui

"Poets are citizens of language."

—Edwin Torres

NASCENT

It begins at a diacritical spark of breath and soma.

Vowel stress nasal enunciation the tenors of existence.

Ictus of *'iiná* inside where *person*

ticks in utero like *tó* rippling skin.

Hitherto by way of *sonus* in a moment in accordance

with vocabulary body forms:

the single *'ii* long interval appends in

muscular tube of *ná*.

See the ink's   flagella zig zag

skirr towards   page ovum

to perforate   its egg coat

fecundate   the nucleus of this

sheet opposite of   black like

static vibrating   epidermis

eardrum.

It's a plash on   parchment sheet

a single drip seep. Ink as semen

      saturates fibrous layers, stimulates

the origin of the length of a tongue,

      igniting between no light and cot-

ton rag paper. The acute cadence

      glisters, a glottal flicker like dotting

the top of an upper stem, head-

      less human silhouette. Throat deep

where the parturition of phrase

      of aphorism   breathes and coos.

Ab ovo there's sound only sound shaping

visible bod and noggin to hear

perspicacity. It is active fro and to

an infinite oscillation of analphabetic

procreation to circumflex: *Díí,* these

pitches of stress these flares over letters

hover, keep in place the strained origin in speech

these newborn glissandos these move-

ments tense and revise type-size

where *diits'a'* designs permanence.

Pronunciation marks are proof

of one's own cultural sentience.

Those authentic reverberations

above the cap height where breath

pressures tongue against teeth,

below the baseline where throat

exhales the long accent vowel,

in that moment it echoes through

nose, quivers as phonemic air:

the ogonek tickle of   łįį'.

Someone once said to debate

oneself is to debate the page.

It's a space a locus of excursus

where vibrations leap between

self and proportion. When one

peers into that leaf mirror

of   white   and   hush,   it   subsumes

thought.   Because   the   word   *I*,

a   reflection   of   the   mind,   is   supple

and   limitless.   To   say   it   means

to   practice   immediacy   but   to   write

it   means   to   construct   perpetuity.

Because within the expanse of page

ego is pro tem like shade produced

by body. And in that movement

when one strokes that single vertical,

descends the line and stipples a dot,

its   inkblood   courses.

A letter on the page affirms the being of *person*.

Per- in accordance with the root

son,

a *prod* and *slit* like an iota contour.

Written: a projection of what occurs instantly in the mind,

our sense of self-*ere*   vibration waves in air

until we materialize   body size between the x-height.

This is how we understand ourselves

through the placement and movement of ink

absorbing into paper.

PAPER MILK

For Chance

Newborn alphabet cries its vowels and the page
nourishes them: *a* opens into a *u*, it becomes a tiny
cup, fills with paper milk; the *e*, too, unfurls to an *o*
and nurses on the colostrum of pulp—thought
attaches sound from *motherese* to thin sheet of
white. Form, a structure of feeling, an instrument
of print means to foster—the verso and recto will
be caretakers of our infant text, as writing develops
calcium to bring life to ink, letters become collagen
of thoughts.

a

is ox head:

dark snout and horn, body blank as milk.   Originates from

measurement of animal to print, first as labor on landscape,

then on page as libel. People create from what their objects

contribute for them. That's why text behaves.   Ox, a living

thing, nonhuman, image of subsistence. It is also on paper a

metaphor.   Sometimes ox will be a loop with an adjacent

vertical stroke or a circle with an arc over it,   indefinite.

b

a single empty room and no door. Cottage, with floor

plan of font, houses bare thought. To see it you will

have to close your right eye and tilt your head

perpendicular to the length of a page. The pupil is

a letter, and the letter is an ink spark—a call-fire

on words to burn in order to comprehend sound. And

sound is flare to awaken the muscles of ocular

movement.

c

bent by page

to form a sling,

the clasp of pap-

er enfolds thought

into type-projectile.

Within word space

it will be an edged

weapon, carved

from ink, an ogive

of tone. It flits as

consonant sign

by jot of a toot,

to volt endlessly

from digraph to

capacitance: a letter

charge, an arc point

to ignite the tongue   to split.

d

a fusiform   thought:

                                  aquatic vertebrate,   caudal fin—

    to cross word,

                              precision movement

      through aquarium alphabet   and ocean map   of folio.

   Senses,   lateral line

           detects tremors in paragraph,

within depth,   white   isolated,   vibrations occur

    forceful

       scintilla of   letter conductivity.

                           Form, less influential than   maneuvering,

                                                          sounds outlast

                              their configurations

                  in book.

So capture

and rest it   in open hand,

let it squirm

                  from lack of paper air,

                        bring close to your ear   take in its   short gasps.

e

on knee to bow, a human figure,　　　prayer at the white altar page.　　　For letters commit our sins,

but in turn redeem us from print.

He wears what appears to be a black shirt and white clerical collar,　　is that why we trust him with our thoughts

to serve as subpoena to the book,　　　and yet, always to disavow a system common to sentence?

That is why we sound out,

　　　　　to spell,

　　　　　　　invoke pause where he's speechless at the end of a word,

　　　　　　　　　to worship in silence.

f

ligaturing to another: its beak posits in capitulum of *i*

to conjoin cursive-like. Letters abbreviate within

each other to equate. Though in its own pictorial

of hook or mace, both ball-peened for ache purpose.

Clouts breathiness against ear with its droplet-shaped

fist. In that a writer at times misshapes letter as tool,

a combo of types espouses inner variables to perceive

textuary whole and not   parts—fuses to extend.

g

from an unfinished circlet or with a trace of another form within,   continuous flexure occurs.

As someone indites the evolution of writing grows,

so to create *g* ink bends sinuously like an ampersand,

curvilinear. Variant between miniscule and majuscule,

how does a letter become another when its origin

is lost? It develops by always being written,

each time its shape requires various perceptions on the page.

I see why revision feels ambit with this one shaped like an inner ear,   listening to my insinuations.

h

forces a vowel to gutturalize,

a harsh vox-tone,   hems off.

Its letter structure as in-between

to guide eye on surface, as fence

ink. Perhaps as checkpoint con-

gests paper to restrict gasps in

etched echo-forms.

   Anaphoric by

syllable for nuance of ear, but by eye

an image, breath ascending a ladder.

WHIT

There's a silence on paper that does not require ears only the reverberation

of a page turning—

      She asks, *so how does it feel to be a letter?*

She waits for him to notice her.   She is exclamation-like

                but upended,   her feet tiptoeing,

                balletic   in her black tutu;

scurrying dashes of ink   calligraphic, as if quill pen

                on parchment   annotating solicitude.

      He replies, "I think of it as a carapace, a place of solitude and cerebration—"

She presses on to prance around him,

but he is ensconced,

his body catafalque as she divulges,

I like that you don't expire.

"—I will not lapse because we are equipoise,

we embody each other like iota,

we are obmutescent, you are verb and I, noun;

when you locomote, your toes traipsing

I feel to urge from my exocarp

to accord my bones to tremble."

JUNCTURE

Each holds either a dot or a comma: the *i* dressed as
magician in white bowtie and black tuxedo pants,
pulls out a period from his top hat and juggles it with
one hand. But the *j* in a black habit kneels like a nun
confined within the solitude of paper, clenches within
her hand a comma shaped cross—to conceal the sign
of sentence.

EMIT

Letters will evade and strive

within the labor of words, under

the weight of ink, of *languish*.

And each alphabet a stapes,

a lilt of sound: curve murmurs

to *O* and straight quivers

in *L*. In that moment, form

intones, letters exist in book,

the cochlea of thought. An impulse

shudders *j*, its bent leg, leaps out

from a sentence, as *i* stridulates

its serif points against paper, a deep

                              trill—silent chirp.

LIMN

It reveals the sketch of letters from meditation: of an
i, a pause between line and dot, or length of the curve
in *j*. Space and stroke determine the ductus of letter.
And when a circle in thought functions only as an
idea, notarized into paper, it becomes a gradation of
pigments, an absent measure of thought, an outline of
the color white.

ETYMON

Sketch the outer edge of

a sound's visible stem

and dot where vowel space

modifies tongue's closing

gesture, variant from the

open swash of *j*.

• • •

Adjacent to each linked

with italic strokes to

ease handwriting

and print, only later

scissioned to distinguish

contexts and phonetics.

• • •

He for the first time

suggests a thought-puzzle:

imaginary, to root in

form of negative sooth, sense.

• • •

Yet, in *self-argument* he

encases his pitch in print,

subjects his *pre-figure* to un-

limit meaning and prescribes

a fixity in formula and folio,

manifests his body as pronoun

dense like ink and   tittle,

idle as period.

k

an open hand—

      another will never recur before *a* or after *o*:

    it is space,   white that occupies.

And underneath,

        it absorbs fluid, dark   until design etiolates.

     An absence of how likely some thing will disappear,

sharp angles indicate pulse   but also indicate its measure   of lifespan,

    how long as surface phenomena will it be print?

          People write and change,   but language when written might not.

1

dark in back
throat hums,

rubs to ridge
alveolar root
of tongue

looms toward
teeth. To feel

sound one must
oral from belly.

Cough up soul-
pulp, evidence
of incorporeal self.

m

a structured fluid speech current, arcs flow to mum,

within its aqueduct ink throbs a motion sensation.

As bone marrow in cavities of skeleton sponge out

vital fluid, or needle point pulls vein into syringe tube.

Breath holds to pronounce its semblance. To exhale

separates nasal tone from print: an influx of throat.

Almost a clog in sentence, puncture-ation break marks

in accidence but only in a momentary *utter*, fluidity quops.

It's an elemental thought from a deep well of apperception,

color- and odor-less in pipelines of mind-perforations.

n

undulates

between

page,   ink: a language

  blood vessel.

Oxygenates   cadence.

            Without it   *being*

            will not have breath.

Write, means to

            place life

              into   book.

Letters live,

   reaffirm   self

within   it.

      An ink vein

      funnels

      plasma thought

      through   word

in moment   one

               pens it.

O

with dark iris, white pupil.

Spatial,

focal point on surface, guides

into white.

Letter hypnotizes to stay

alive after meaning fades.

Bold light

projects outward; depth pressure,

squint periphery.

Singes pretext from nerve sight

to hue of page margin.

Paper cornea

insulates thought from pale

liquid burn

of aperture letter:

a calcine color, to ash bleach.

EMPTY SET

Vacant folio,　　　　　middle of an unwritten;

coaxial *o* rolls out from its shape:

　　　　　unoccupied but

designed by　　inaudible flashes of *colorless*.

In the depths of paper, underneath

text; what was before　　　　a blank,

another layer of spotless pulp. Circle

out of its dermis ink: human bulb, skull light.

Where the substance of thought

enlightens　　　　the narrative of bone,

skeleton according to speech;

of being alive within empty set.

Like a shape of   sound before

ink forms, before structured print

writhes through and out. Curly brackets

enclose sibilant: an *s*, a phonetic infection.

But a writer corrects what it hears, forgets

in there where   ink absorbs paper, evolves

into written fungic. A spore of alphabet cannot

be sterilized with revision;   so one creates

a circumference   around the letter

to entrap, to press   its outbreak of silence.

BLOCK CIPHER

Under diagram   of a letter-less paragraph,

block white.   Silent quadrates,   grid   imperceptible

where the arrangement   cross-puzzles itself.

Blank words   equidistant   by page   flectional   by print.

Structure of paper   exists to limit   *communicatio*

of sound   of silence;   how word-types   appear,

how fonts   distinguish   an ipseity of language.

The pages' margins   shape set-text   a voice unwrit;

contains unseen   accent,   pressure wave code.

Where breath   within paper   functions   a sensation thought,

actions   charge   form.   Without

a point   an *i*   will forget   its direction,   or a *j*

with its curve   will not show   its breadth   of line.

UNWRITTEN

Excavate what appears to be an *O*

    remove its tiny white cranium.

Within text there is extinction,   bone-shaped artifacts.

Enough to reveal part of what covers a skull,   to scrape

out its ink   with a trowel: loop of an unfinished

alphabet,

    C bent in an incomplete circle.

    _____is not vacant only quiet and nameless,

    unwritten in the depths of the page,   an unswathed sound.

See the skeleton of its head,   how it grins,

how its sentence teeth   clench

          until it fractures a piece of a letter.

          Dig the rest of its design   from layered page,

          chip at its body   until bone exposes;

          fold paper in half   and feel it separate

          from its form.   Chart its ink structure,

          that framework of a word   just a body bag,

          that is where the calcium hardens

CONFIGURATION

Lumbar curve is subject,

predicate, as thoracic curve,

and cervical curve, verb:

the notochord of thought.

Its dark nonsecular body

wears an   ink cassock.

To claim a kind of priesthood

functioning through gospel

sonority, converting syntax

of the ear   to transmute.

That limbless sign   head

disjoints   its form to set

apart—strip it clean of ink-cloth

reveal   spinal syntax

on the scaffold of   page,

its head   a bone dot

backbone   a sentence.

SENTENTIAL

At the end of an expired grammatical idea, a full stop

will augment an outline of a dried skeleton.

        Lay it out on an examination page:

        align the remains of accidence

        rudiments of syntax to re-ossify these

thought-bones. Affix its appendicular subject and axial verb

the framework of a vox unit:

                with ink-ossein

                etch serifs in-between,

                draw lacrimal bone-commas

                to *inchoate* its grammar joints   and witness its assemblage discourse—

DISSOCIATE

Rip vertebral column from q

snap the ribs off x

from its ink skin pull out the skull of e.

This is why we disembody form from flesh,

   we divest.

How does a letter disjoin itself

when it imprisons its self?

The persistence of composition means

nothing without the shapes of letters.

Because they must wear dark fabrics,

pale neck cloths—but now *j*

dressed in black scrubs,

surgical mask, grasps a dark scalpel.

She will dissect the disposable head,

so next time   you see *i*,

                                   only the body, dotless.

AMBIGUATE

The downward stroke   a *vertical bar* which sustains: *piece/fraction* of text.

To project dash-shadow between aposiopesis and imagination   a *line segment* at both ends

links to its colorant mediation.   Then an *interpunct*, a pigment of the page: a midpoint

of terminus.   Next the space of lowercase body and dot: a *twist axis* of silence.   Functional

white loops nonstop, an ongoing chronograph click to zero   an *apparent horizon* to brood

our consciousness time and again.   Punctuation as psychography as illumination   a mark

feels   punctilious and autonomous   like tail-shedding   a limb still composing.

FINIS

A sound-loop hangs from the white gallows of the page:

     letter *j* strung up,

               the crook of her foot postmortem—

               leg sway.

       Mouth retches

                   a vowel   *round o*

      then from the roof

                    gasps   *a dark l slung.*

  Is not innocent:

         the *i* with a white noose

         also around his neck,

         blindfolded, asphyxiated.

Spaces within   words are   miniature knots

that suspend letters—

        the paper

               always tightening.

TO UNCOLOR

Use paper tweezers pinch free the ink delicately like pin-bones from a fish. Pull out *stems, cross bars, ascenders,* and *descenders.* Now, place the page inside a crucible, fill with chlorine and bring to a boil. Add a measure of borax to help cleanse *serif* blotches. Place a lid atop of it, wait momentarily. When edges of type are *anti-aliased* the limits of language restrain. In the meantime think of *folio* steam burns, its layers blistering lampblack, color fluid discharging and then liquid parching. Do not damage the surface—a smudge is immutable. Even its dense sentences and paragraphs should begin to degrade as the pulp loosens. Watch as the *letter* disarticulates from its *baseline* like a pivotal joint unhitching from a spine through maceration: it's in that moment print attains a satori of blankness, permutes the paper of complete space.

CEPHALIC

I place a black cloth the size of a dot over his head. Wrap his entire miniscule body with a thread of my black hair. He lies there on a white sheet of paper and squirms like a dark cocoon, thinks he is going to transform. The letter, when it begins to lose color in a book never opened, becomes a macula in thought. And when read through the lens of a decimal point: see its dark fleck of a cranium, see expendable language—grab the letter *j* next to him, hold it like a tiny black scythe, behead the *i*, and watch its dot head roll to the back of a sentence.

ACKNOWLEDGMENTS

I want to thank my family: Mae White, Ty Johnson, Gabrial Johnson and Sandie Johnson, for their undying support and love. To my friends who continue to encourage and challenge me: Sherwin Bitsui, dg nanouk okpik, Santee Frazier, Arthur Sze and Jon Davis. To my peers and professors from graduate school: Jonathan Redhorse, Christine Gardiner, Linnea Ogden, Feliz Molina, Thibault Raoult, Carlos Lara, Pablo Lopez, Michael Keenan, Sarah Stone, Amanda Katz, Shya Scanlon, Forrest Gander, C.D. Wright, Keith Waldrop, John Cayley, and Brian Evenson. To everyone who has in some form or fashion assisted me in any way at all, you know who you are. And lastly, thank you to the mother of my child, Layli Long Soldier, and to my kid, Chance Ohitika Alexie White, for always being the light and center of my existence.

My grateful acknowledgments to the following journals and magazines for which these poems first appeared sometimes in earlier versions: "Whit" in the *American Indian Culture and Research Journal*; "l," "m," "n," and "o" in *Bombay Gin*; "To Uncolor" in *The Drunken Boat*; "Empty Set," "f," and "h" in *The Florida Review*; "a," "e," and "k" in *The Kenyon Review*; "c" and "Finis" in *Omnidawn Poetry Feature Blog*; "Unwritten" and "Paper Milk" in *Oregon Literary Review*; "Cephalic" in *Salt Hill Journal*; "b" and "Juncture" in *Sentence: A Journal of Prose Poetics*; "Limn," "Emit," and "Dissociate" in *Superstition Review*; and "d" and "g" in *Talking Stick Native Arts Quarterly*.

My deepest appreciation goes out to the Lannan Foundation for giving me the time and space to write and finish this book. Also, to Marilyn Nelson at Soul Mountain Retreat and the Bread Loaf Writers Conference, thank you so much for your generosity and help.

Orlando White is from Tółikan, Arizona. He is Diné of the Naaneesht'ézhi Tábaahí and born for the Naakai Diné'e. He is the author of two books of poetry, *Bone Light* (Red Hen Press), which Kazim Ali described as a "careful excavation on language and letters and the physical body" and *LETTERRS* (Nightboat Books) which received the Poetry Center Book Award. He teaches at Diné College and lives in Diné Nation.

ABOUT NIGHTBOAT BOOKS

Nightboat Books, a nonprofit organization, seeks to develop audiences for writers whose work resists convention and transcends boundaries. We publish books rich with poignancy, intelligence, and risk. Please visit nightboat.org to learn more about us and how you can support our future publications.

The following individuals have supported the publication of this book. We thank them for their generosity and commitment to the mission of Nightboat Books:

Elizabeth Motika
Benjamin Taylor

In addition, this book has been made possible, in part, by grants from The Fund for Poetry, the National Endowment for the Arts, and the New York State Council on the Arts Literature Program.